Music Explorer
Project Book

Richard McNicol

Apollo Trust
in association with Oxford University Press

Outline instructions for these projects are also available in the form of photocopiable pupils' sheets. Subject to availability these may be purchased from the publisher:

Apollo Trust
145 Park Road
Buxton
Derbyshire SK17 6SW
England

tel/fax 01298 79598

With thanks to Pauline Allen, Frances Williams and all teachers who have
    helped to pilot these projects

Published in Great Britain by Apollo Trust, 145 Park Road, Buxton,
    Derbyshire, SK17 6SW
© 1996 Richard McNicol
ISBN 0 9528934 0 1

Edited and designed by Peter Nickol
Cover design by Premm Design
Illustrations by Liz Silk
Printed by Buxton Press

Contents

Introduction

Progression and Continuity

Introduction

What better way could there be to get inside the music of a great composer than by using that composer's musical ideas yourself? The ideas for the projects in this book come from the music of the twelve world-famous composers whose music is explored in the London Symphony Orchestra *Music Explorer* video.

This book may be used with or without the *Music Explorer* video. If you decide to use it on its own, your pupils will, at the end of each project, have the satisfaction of performing a well-structured piece of music that they themselves have composed. Used in conjunction with the video, they will appraise the music on the video with a perceptiveness gained from practical experience.

All the projects involve pupils in composing and performing, and are designed to have a wide range of application in the classroom. The primary school class-teacher with little or no musical knowledge will feel as comfortable with them as the secondary school music specialist; primary school pupils will have as much fun doing them as will pupils working towards GCSE or Standard Grade.

Structure – the way musical ideas are developed and assembled to build a piece of music – is fundamental to each project. In addition, all the projects expose the pupils to a variety of basic musical elements and techniques. Many are designed for pupils working in groups so that discussion can fertilise invention and many hands can produce complex and rewarding pieces of music. Others enable pupils to explore musical ideas on their own or in pairs. Where suggested you may photocopy the text so that pupils can work from it at their own speed.

Alternatively, photocopiable pupils' sheets are available covering *all* the projects. These – like assembly instructions – outline the main stages in the project, and also include such diagrams etc. as may be necessary.

To help you to plan progression in your teaching the projects become gradually more demanding. Musical concepts are introduced, then consolidated in successive projects (see *Progression and Continuity*, opposite). Where appropriate I have used standard Italian musical terms (indicated in italics beside the English equivalent) so that pupils will gradually become familiar with the international terminology of music.

Above all these projects are designed to make music in your classroom an exciting and fulfilling experience. I hope you enjoy them.

Richard McNicol

Progression and Continuity

All the projects involve inventing and structuring simple musical materials. All involve performing. All involve focused listening. Some of the specific learning outcomes of each project are listed below – but it should be borne in mind that the projects can be used in different ways and at different levels to teach many different things.

Participants in the projects will learn about:

Groups: projects 2, 4, 6, 10, 12, 17, 20
Groups/class: 1, 3, 5, 7, 13, 15, 16
Pairs: 21, 22   *Groups/pairs:* 14
Individually/in fours: 8   *Pairs/in fours:* 11
Individually or pairs: 9
In threes: 18   *In fours:* 23
In eights: 24   *In eights/class:* 19

1 Spring
Inventing a tune to a poem, listening and responding, turning the sounds of nature into music, singing

2 Dreams in a Silent Landscape
Creating atmosphere, background and foreground, tunes, dynamics, birdsong

3 The Lost Planet
Creating atmosphere, background and foreground, texture, timbre, contrast

4 Colours and Textures
Texture, rhythm, timbre, chords, clusters, colour, dynamics, ostinato

5 Rainbow Migration
Texture, background and foreground, timbre, dynamics, colour

6 Musical Portraits
Creating music from limited materials, rhythm, ostinato

7 Special Day Collage
Creating music from limited materials, contrast, texture, density, pacing

8 Taking Turns
Solo and accompaniment, developing musical material, dynamics, contrast

9 Shaping the Tune
Inventing tunes, melodic shape, answering phrases

10 Perform this Graphic Score
Tune and accompaniment, developing musical material, graphic score, texture

11 Shadow Dances
Tune and accompaniment with dance, intervals

12 Disruptive Behaviour
Tune and accompaniment, rhythm, imitation, tune on tune, drone, contrast, dynamics

13 Decoration Day
Tune and accompaniment, rhythm on rhythm, atmosphere

14 Stretch – and Relax
Melodic shape, tension and relaxation, following notation

15 Power Machine
Rhythm, developing musical material, sequences, rounds, blocks of sound, dynamics, singing

16 Fives
Rhythm on rhythm, duration, developing musical material, layers of tune, contrasting tempi

17 Aggressive Gestures
Rhythm and duration, tune and accompaniment, imitation, texture, drone, ostinato, contrast, dynamics

18 Musical Tennis
Imitation, music in thirds, developing musical material

19 Sequences and Signatures
Sequences, call and response, drone, singing

20 Grand Bathing Ceremony
Tune and accompaniment, rounds, texture, rhythm

21 Miniature Jigsaws
Imitation, tune on tune

22 Follow my Leader
Rounds, inventing a tune to words, drone, singing

23 Gossip, Gossip
How a fugue works, sequences, rhythm, dynamics

24 A Flying Bed
Imitation, developing musical material, tunes, dynamics, pauses, contrast, singing

Project 1
Spring

1 Write a poem about Spring

Ask for a list of things that signal the coming of Spring; then develop this into a short, one-verse poem. As suggestions are offered, write the evolving poem on the board.

2 Invent a Spring song

When everyone is satisfied with the poem, invite someone to sing the first line, using whatever tune comes into their head. Everyone else must sing it back. Who would like to offer an alternative tune for the first line? Again, everyone else sings it back.

When there is agreement on a musical phrase that suits the first line of the poem, sing it several times to memorise it. Then move onto the second line of the poem – and so on to the end.

When the song is complete, record it. The recording will be a useful aide-mémoire.

3 Make the sound of birds singing

Many birds – cuckoos for example – repeat the same simple phrase. Others, like blackbirds, have a more complex repertoire of phrases. As a demonstration, ask someone to invent a very simple birdsong using only three notes. It can be sung, whistled, or played on an instrument. Ask someone else to echo it exactly from the other side of the room.

Choose three more pairs to invent more birdsong. When the songs are ready, ask the four different species to sing whenever they wish. Each bird must be answered by its partner. Try it with eyes closed, so that each performer must listen very carefully for the right song to answer.

Next, everyone else forms similar groups of six or eight, likewise dividing into pairs to invent more birdsongs. Eventually all the groups can combine to make one glorious dawn chorus. If chaos results, suggest that each pair sings only twice during the piece.

Record the performance. Can the clarity of the piece be further improved so that every birdsong is clearly heard?

▢ If possible watch Music Explorer Programme 1, from 13 to 27

Vivaldi tells us that this music represents birdsong. It doesn't imitate birds, but the violinists do play short, repetitive phrases, and one player imitates another.

4 Turn the birdsong into instrumental music

Go back into groups to invent music that *behaves* like birdsong without *imitating* birdsong. Short phrases, repetition, one performer imitating another, will be important ideas to remember.

5 Make a musical picture of streams burbling and gentle breezes blowing

This is a new section of music. Ask the groups to use tuned instruments (for example xylophones, recorders, violins – or voices) to create the sound of a stream burbling gently along its shallow bed. They must always move to adjacent notes – leaps are forbidden. Here too they are inventing music that *behaves* like a burbling stream.

Then add music like gentle breezes blowing.

⬜ Watch Programme 1 again, from 31 to 36

This is Vivaldi's stream and breeze music. Watch the violinists' fingers. The music always moves to next-door notes, giving a gentle undulating effect.

At 37 the violins sigh smoothly (this is the wind) while the basses burble on beneath.

6 Make a sudden thunder storm

This is a job for one group only! Ask them to invent a musical thunder storm with flashes of lightning and crashes of thunder. Could they also add some musical rain? Send them away to invent their storm while everyone else moves on to stage 7.

7 Assemble the musical pictures to make one piece of Spring music, using the song as a 'ritornello'

You have three musical pictures (birds; stream and breezes; storm), and these will form the fillings between a chorus or *ritornello* which returns again and again; this is the 'Spring song' (stages 1–2).

Decide which group will perform which musical picture. If there are more than three groups, there can be two sections of bird-music or stream-music. Everyone sings the song-ritornello.

Now set the task of assembling a piece of Spring music. Don't forget to save a place for the storm group when they return. If (for instance) there are four groups, a plan of the piece might look like this:

Ritornello (Spring song – everyone)
Birds (group 1)
Ritornello
Stream and breezes (group 2)
Ritornello
Storm (group 3)
Ritornello
More birds (different ones: group 4)
Ritornello

⬜ Watch Programme 1 right through. Can you see the connections?

Vivaldi's music is also in ritornello form. The opening music, Vivaldi's Spring song, returns after each musical description. In the score he writes the words 'Spring is here and with it happiness'.

Notice the thunder (44), played *tremolando* (by trembling the bows on the strings), and the rushing scales that represent lightning (45), followed by heavy rain (starting at 47) – a torrent of notes from the solo violin punctuated by continuing growls of thunder.

Vivaldi writes two sections of birdsong music, the second starting at 59.

For a more detailed look at the piece, and this performance of it, see the *Music Explorer* guidebook.

Project 2
Dreams in a Silent Landscape

1 Imagine a wild, uncharted land. It is night, and very still. A group of explorers, lost and weary, are sunk in troubled sleep. Invent a dream sequence for this scene, using only voices

Divide the class into groups to create this scene. The audience must get an impression of the dreams of the explorers disturbing the stillness of the wilderness.

Imagine that the scene is being created for radio. In radio drama, sounds are used inventively to conjure up images in the listeners' minds.

Impose these three rules:
- Use voices only.
- The dream fragments must be very short.
- No snores are allowed.

Perform the dream sequences. Did the groups manage to capture the sense of stillness in the wilderness?

2 Concentrate on the background

Now that the class has made a start, help them to develop their ideas. Concentrate first on the darkness and stillness. In a television programme things can happen in silence. On radio, when the audience can't see what is going on, silence is difficult to handle. Its place is often taken by music, which creates atmosphere and fills in the background.

Go back into groups and use instruments (and perhaps some singing) to evoke the stillness of the wilderness at night. This is the background to which the fragments of dreams will later be added.

If guidance is needed, suggest that the stillness might be portrayed by long, quiet sounds that hardly move.

3 Add the dream fragments to the still background

Use the same vocal dream fragments as before. Think carefully about the order of the dream fragments. Perhaps one of them should be repeated, or should return again towards the end to give the sequence some kind of structure.

Be sure it is clear to the listener which are background sounds and which are dream fragments, perhaps by making the background very still and the dreaming more restless.

Record the performances. How effective would they be in a radio drama?

4 Change the dream fragments into purely musical ideas

In place of dreams, ask the groups to 'paint' a new set of ingredients onto their musical canvas:
- sounds heard in the countryside

(particularly birdsong)

- sounds from an army barracks (bugle calls or fanfares)
- a short section of sad tune

These different ideas might be represented by short sections of tune, rhythms, or simply evocative combinations of sounds. They should be short – the longest no more than 15 seconds. Instead of voices, ask them to use instruments.

5 Build a musical structure

When the ideas are ready, the most important part of composing can begin – building the ingredients into an effective piece of music. A number of important decisions must be made about the overall structure of the piece:

1 How should it begin?
2 Should the fragments come one after another or should they overlap? In what order should they come?
3 Should the volume stay the same throughout, should it start quietly and build up to a climax, or would some other dynamic shape work well?
4 How should the piece finish?

When the project is completed, watch Music Explorer Programme 5, from the beginning to 458. What connections can you see?

Point out how Mahler creates stillness by bringing the slow-moving opening to a standstill (at 430); the string players simply hold long notes.

Mahler's musical ideas represent memories from his childhood:

430, 436   fanfares (Mahler lived near an army camp)
439, 452   birdsong (he loved the countryside)
444–452   melancholy melody (Mahler suffered from debilitating bouts of melancholia)

Draw attention to the structure of this section of the symphony:

428   stillness then activity (fanfares 430–435)
435   stillness then activity (fanfares and birdsong 437–443)
444   melancholy
448   gradually back to activity (birdsong 452–458)

Project 3
The Lost Planet

1 Write a description of a cold and distant planet

When Holst composed 'The Planets' he wrote seven pieces of music: Mars, Venus, Mercury, Jupiter, Saturn, Uranus and Neptune. Although the astronomer Lowell had predicted the existence of a ninth planet (Earth being one of the eight, of course), Pluto was not discovered until 1930. Now we know that Pluto exists – very small, and so far from the sun that it is perpetually dark and icily cold. Scientists might tell us that no life could exist in such a place, but do we really believe them?

Ask each member of the class to imagine they have discovered a new planet. What name would they give it? Ask them to write a description of their planet. Perhaps they would also like to paint a view of the surface of the planet.

2 Create an icy, alien soundscape

Imagine a science-fiction film. The space probe has landed and its viewer scans the planet's surface. We must compose film-music for this scene. What sort of sounds should we use?

Sparse, resonant sounds, and plenty of silence, will create a feeling of stillness. Regular rhythm is more likely to create a feeling of activity.

Divide the class into groups and ask them to use a mixture of tuned and untuned instruments, and their voices, to capture the chilling cold of the planet without disturbing its lonely stillness. Try, for example, cymbal, Indian bells, recorder, glockenspiel, chime bars, triangle.

You could ask each group to write a description of their planet on a piece of paper. Then, if you write these on the board, listeners could subsequently try to match each piece of music to one of the descriptions.

Each group performs to the class. Invite constructive criticism. Were the sounds truly cold-sounding? Did the music capture the stillness of the planet? Was the way it was *performed* still?

Ask the groups to spend a further few minutes perfecting their music.

3 Put the music of all the groups together

Ask the class to find a way of combining their music to make one large soundscape. They must still perform as groups, and the music must still sound cold and still. Point out that it may be necessary to do some pruning so that the music doesn't become too busy if the groups overlap.

Encourage them to make concrete decisions. Which group starts? Should more than one group play at the same time? How should the piece finish?

If performers need to share instruments,

they can sit together even if they are in different groups. They can still watch and play with their own group from a distance.

4 Make something new happen – something unexpected!

Ask each group to create an unexpected happening on the planet, perhaps the arrival of aliens, a space monster, a volcano erupting. The event must be described in music and it must last no longer than 30 seconds.

5 Add the unexpected events to the icy soundscape

The class now has a background texture of icy music, and several musical events. The task now is to use this musical material to build one piece of music.

Ask for suggestions for an order, and write them on the board. As soon as the order is complete, try it out, and if possible record it. Then discuss its strengths and weaknesses. Discussion is worthwhile, but better to try things out than discuss them for too long. When ideas are quickly tried out we soon discover what works and what does not.

If the class can produce music that works well without the need to explain that it describes a distant planet, they have succeeded very well indeed!

▢ If possible watch Music Explorer Programme 10, from 96

In Programme 10, Holst creates music that is eerie and still by making the deepest-sounding instruments in the orchestra creep around adjacent notes. The violins add to the atmosphere by playing *tremolando* (trembling the bows on the strings).

Then Programme 5, from 428 to 533

Holst's music is about anger and fear of impending war, not about a cold distant planet. Neither is Mahler's music in Programme 5. But there is something truly chilly about the music from 428 to 458. Point out the stillness of the long string notes, and the way the fanfares and birdcalls break in without warning. Then fast-forward to 496. After an intense outburst the music again becomes still. More long notes; then at 519 a startling outburst from the violas. Finish watching at 533.

Finally, watch Programme 11 from 90 to 123, and from 228 to 252

Here are two sections of extraordinarily spooky music; watch carefully how it is done.

Project 4
Colours and Textures

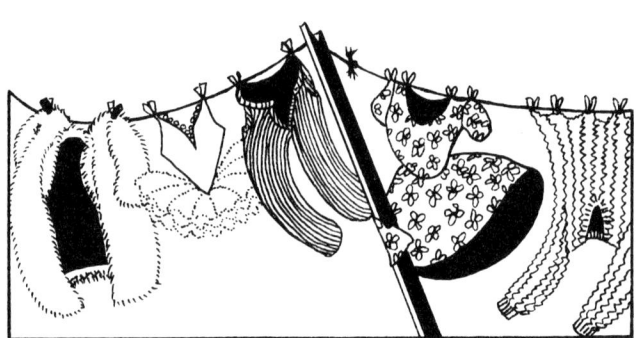

Preparation

Many of the projects in this book are quite highly structured, specifying carefully the musical materials to be used. This project allows more freedom. Give each group the appropriate guidelines (photocopy them if you wish) and leave them to create the detail and structure of the music for themselves.

Your help may be needed when all the groups come together to make one large piece.

The first stage of the project could be viewed as preparation – sorting all available instruments into families – but the class may benefit by participating in this activity.

The last two families listed below – 'blown' and 'string' – are for those who are learning instruments. Putting them with each other can give them an opportunity to work at their own speed, as a change from working in mixed-ability groups.

Arrange all the instruments in families

1 untuned: wooden and skin
including claves, drums, woodblocks, guiros
2 untuned: metal
including triangles, Indian bells, sleigh bells, cymbals, wind-chimes
3 tuned: wooden
including xylophones, tone bars
4 tuned: metal
including glockenspiels, chime bars, metallophones

5 blown
including recorders, flutes, clarinets, trumpets, bottles
6 string
including violins, cellos, guitars, autoharps, zithers

Form a group of players for each family of instruments

Group 1: untuned wooden and skin instruments

These make short, percussive sounds, and are often used as rhythmic instruments. Invent a *rhythmic* piece of music in which:
* nobody plays *all* the time
* different rhythms play at the same time
* there are contrasting loud and quiet sections
* each performer has a chance to be a soloist

Group 2: untuned metal instruments

This group contains some of the most magical of all sounds: the glistening ringing sound of Indian bells, the swish of a cymbal hit with a soft beater, the sparkling shimmer of wind-chimes. Make a *magical* piece of music in which:
* every sound can be heard clearly
* there is a moment when the sound of each instrument can be enjoyed *alone*

- sounds are only combined in the most delicate way possible
- there is *one* very loud moment

Group 3: tuned wooden instruments

When a xylophone is played with hard beaters it sounds brittle and aggressive; with soft beaters, smooth and mellow. Tone-bars (if you have them) are rich and deep.

Invent a piece that makes the most of the *different sounds* that can be made on tuned wooden instruments, making sure that:

- your music flows from beginning to end, without gaps
- no more than three people play at once
- the listeners have time to notice and appreciate each new kind of sound you use
- the piece sounds carefully put together – not as if you are experimenting and making it up as you go along

Group 4: tuned metal instruments

All tuned metal instruments make resonant sounds – sharp and brilliant or, if you use soft beaters, warm and glowing. Compose a piece of music made of *flurries of sound* with long silences in between. That way, the sound of the flurries can be heard ringing on each time you stop playing. Make sure that:

- the music has *no beat* and *no tune*
- there is plenty of contrast between high and low sounds, loud and quiet, fast-moving and slow-moving, etc.
- the silences feel as if they are part of the piece

Group 5: blown instruments

We normally start learning woodwind and brass instruments by playing tunes. But this project is not about tunes, it is about the *different coloured sound* that each different wind instrument makes. Make a piece out of *long notes*, by:

- contrasting one colour of sound with another
- building up chords or *clusters* of long notes
- making some loud and some very quiet music
- adding *one short section* of melody

Group 6: string instruments

Some string instruments are played with a bow, others are plucked or strummed. In this project we will use *plucked and strummed sounds only*. When you create your piece, make sure that:

- an ostinato runs all the way through the piece, played by one or more people
- sometimes the music sounds very busy
- sometimes it sounds lonely
- at one moment during the piece everyone strums together very loudly

If possible watch Music Explorer Programme 11

In his *Concerto for Orchestra* Bartók set out to show groups of instruments doing some of the things they do best:

8–24	bassoons playing poised, bouncy music
25–44	oboes playing crisply and elegantly
45–57	clarinets showing their wide dynamic range
60–86	flutes playing fast and fluently
90–120	trumpets, muted and snarling
123–158	the smooth sound of a complete brass section

The strings, normally the most prominent part of the orchestra, are here used to accompany.

Project 5
Rainbow Migration

Preparation

Set up five pentatonic scales on resonant instruments (metallophone, chime bars, large glockenspiel, bass xylophone, keyboard) so that each group has at least one instrument. Take off the bars that are not needed and use stickers, if necessary, to mark the notes on keyboards.

> *group 1:* C D E G A
> *group 2:* C♯ D♯ F♯ G♯ B♭
> *group 3:* D E G A B
> *group 4:* E♭ F G B♭ C
> *group 5:* E F♯ A B C♯

These scales have been chosen for the fresh-sounding contrasts they will give when the groups come together to make one piece (stage 4).

You may photocopy the project and give a copy to each group. Stages 1–3 are straightforward and should require little teacher input, but help will probably be needed with stage 4.

1 Make a wash of sound

This is like making a colour-wash background when you are going to paint a picture. Try to make the wash of sound as smooth and as beautiful as possible, using all the notes of your pentatonic scale. Think carefully about what sort of beaters you are going to use on the percussion instruments, and which keyboard sounds will be most effective.

2 Make the sounds of a migration

Migration happens all over the world. Many creatures migrate in search of food. People are forced to migrate by natural disasters and war. Birds migrate as the seasons change.

Use your voices and untuned percussion instruments (drums, woodblocks, guiros, maracas, etc.) to make the sounds of a migration. Don't make them too noisy, for they will be combined with the wash of sound. Use your sounds to create a delicate piece of music. Put your sounds together carefully. Remember that composing is building a satisfying musical structure out of sounds, rather like carefully choosing the bricks, wood and glass, then building your own special house.

Organise the sounds of your migration into a shape that will make sense to someone listening. For example, migrating geese may first be heard in the distance. As they get closer they become louder, then when they have passed the sound gradually dies away.

In the next stage of the project you will perform the migration music and the wash of sound at the same time, so make sure there are always some members of the group free to continue playing the wash.

3 Add the migration music to the wash of sound

When we put one piece of music on top of another we must take care that the effect doesn't confuse the listeners. Decide which is the more important, the wash of sound or the migration music. Then use dynamics (loudness and quietness) to make sure that the listeners will be able to hear clearly the most important details of your music.

4 Combine all the groups' music to make a Rainbow Migration

Musicians often use the word 'colour' to describe the contrasting sounds of different instruments. For example, we say that the sound of a xylophone is a different colour from the sound of a glockenspiel. This project is called 'Rainbow Migration' because each group's migration music is accompanied by a differently coloured wash of sound – using a different instrument and a different set of notes.

And the music can migrate from one group to another. Perform the migration pieces in succession. Try groups 1 to 5 in order, then try dotting around: group 1 followed by group 4 followed by group 2 etc. Listen to the effect as each new wash of sound starts. Which order does everyone find most effective?

This new combined piece must be put together in the same careful way as the individual group pieces were structured. You may decide to start with a group that is really quiet, then follow it with a loud group. Or you may wish to save the quiet group for a moment of magic in the middle of the piece. Contrast and dynamics can transform a piece of music.

When the final performance has taken place, watch Music Explorer Programme 7

Ravel's music is not about migration, but he does use pentatonic scales to create the wonderful washes of sound that accompany his tunes.

1–8   Some of the cellos shimmer (*tremolando*) and some pluck (*pizzicato*). And listen to the smooth sounds of the wind instruments in the background.

83–92   The strings hold long notes and the double basses and harp play a gentle ostinato to accompany the clarinet tune.

Notice how Ravel uses the colours of the different instruments:

38–55   the tune changes colour from the flute (38) to the cor anglais (42) and back, again and again

95   the colour of the clarinet is combined with the colour of the celeste (they play the same tune, but two notes apart, as a round)

142   the fast tune returns played by celeste; then, at 149 the colour changes as the piccolo is added

Sometimes Ravel makes sudden changes of dynamic:

24   a sudden change from quiet to loud, then back to quiet at 25

and at other times the change is gradual:

57–65   a gradual build-up (*crescendo*) from quiet (*piano*) to loud (*forte*)

69–82   the reverse: *diminuendo* from *forte* to *piano*

Turn to page 37 in the Music Explorer guidebook to see how carefully Ravel builds his musical materials into a symmetrical structure.

Project 6
Musical Portraits

1 Describe somebody in one short sentence

Think about people's individuality. We all look different, but what often makes more impression on others is the way we behave.

Give the class an example by describing two characteristics of an imaginary child you know:

'She skips around all the time and every so often she sneezes.'

2 Turn the description into music

Invite someone to use a woodblock to describe the imaginary child skipping around. Does the class agree that the music skips, or can they suggest a more effective way of making skipping music?

Ask someone else to use a xylophone to add an ostinato that fits with the skipping music. Perhaps someone else would like to add a second ostinato.

'Every so often she sneezes.' Perhaps she has a cold, or hay fever. Should the sneeze be added on an instrument – perhaps something that produces a short, explosive sound? Or would the class prefer an actual sneeze?

Where should the sneeze fit into the skipping music? Should it happen while the music is skipping along, or should the skipping music stop first? How often should the sneeze be heard?

If possible watch Music Explorer Programme 12, from the beginning to 110. Suppose this were a portrait of someone. What sort of person would it be?

Think of some adjectives to describe the music.

There are many appropriate adjectives – fast, loud, aggressive, relentless, rough, serious, brutal, breathless. Some of these accurately describe the man as well – for this is a portrait of Joseph Stalin.

The music starts with short, brittle notes separated by gaps. At 7 this brutal, disjointed music forms the accompaniment to a strong tune, which at 21 takes off suddenly at a frantic gallop. The tune contrasts sharply with its accompaniment.

Draw attention to the way Shostakovich uses the instruments. Violinists attack their strings aggressively with their bows. At 31 a snare drum interrupts abruptly. At 67 the brass instruments sound arrogant and powerful.

3 Write your own two-line description of a friend

Ask everyone to write a sympathetic, two-line description of someone they know, *concentrating on two characteristics*. Some may like to read out their descriptions.

4 Turn the description into a musical portrait

Divide into groups to take one of the descriptions and turn it into a musical portrait. Remind the groups that they are restricted to *two characteristics only*.

When they have decided how to turn each characteristic into music, remind them how the skipping and sneezing ideas were assembled to build a whole piece of music. Now they must find a way of using their own two ingredients to build an effective musical structure.

Watch Programme 12 again, this time right through. How does Shostakovich develop his ingredients?

The opening tune is developed into fast-moving music by using the same musical shape at twice the speed (from 21).

At 31 Shostakovich starts all over again. This is the same opening music but *reorchestrated*. Now the horns play the accompaniment and the violins play the tune (from 37).

Notice how the short trumpet phrase (67–69) is developed into something longer. At 70 it is repeated and extended by adding a shape (73–75) that was first heard at 3. 86 is the same rhythm, but instead of descending from the third note, it rises.

The block of music from 115 to 131 is played first by strings, then wind (from 132). Then from 163 it is played by the whole orchestra. And throughout the double basses play an ostinato (watch them from 112 to 121) to tie the whole structure together.

Of course, Shostakovich uses more than two ingredients for his musical portrait of Joseph Stalin – he is after all writing a long symphonic movement.

Project 7
Special Day Collage

1 Write about a special day

Talk about special days. Some are obvious: Divali, Christmas Day, birthdays, Sports Day, a visit to the sea. Some are more private but no less special.

What makes a day special? Ask everyone to write a short account of a special day they can remember, and read some of them out loud.

2 Make an art collage

Ask each person to paint or draw something from their own special day – not the whole day, just one ingredient.

Then help the class to assemble the pictures. Pay particular attention to:

- *Contrast* A colourful picture beside a quiet one, a bold image beside subtle detail
- *Density* One picture partly covering another, a group of pictures clustered together
- *Structure* The overall shape of the collage, for instance a crowd of pictures in the middle and a few well spaced out round the periphery

These will be important considerations when the class comes to assemble a musical collage.

3 Create the ingredients for a musical collage

Each individual contributed a picture to the art collage, but for the musical collage each ingredient will be created by a group. Ask each group to turn *one single memory* of a special day into music. They might choose sounds which were originally musical – 'Happy Birthday to you', instruments tuning up before a concert, fairground music, disco music – or they might choose other sounds or sound effects – animal sounds from a zoo visit, calls and laughter from a beach game.

Make a time-limit of fifteen seconds for each ingredient. They may have to prune their pieces to achieve this – a good musical discipline in itself. And to encourage careful decision-making, stipulate that each piece must be identical each time it is performed.

Otherwise leave the groups free to choose and develop their own ideas. The effectiveness of the collage will depend more on its structure than on the sophistication of the individual ingredients.

4 Assemble the collage, with careful attention to contrast, density and structure

Invite each group to perform its miniature to the class. Everyone must listen carefully; they will have to decide which element will go where in the collage. Musical collages can all too easily sound like a series of pieces performed one after the other – not a collage at all. The finished piece must run continuously, as a single performance.

Help the class to establish an order, paying particular attention to the *pacing* of the music. Pacing – the rate at which the music unfolds – is like the pacing of a good lesson; at times we move forward quickly, at times we linger over a point, sometimes we stimulate the class, sometimes we calm them. Good pacing will help to hold people's attention.

The very same points that were highlighted when making the art collage will affect the pacing of the music:

- *Contrast* Vigorous sounds might follow still sounds; a short fragment might follow a longer one.
- *Density* One fragment might be interrupted or overlapped by another; at some point, everyone might perform simultaneously.
- *Structure* The overall shape of the music. Ask everyone to suggest ways of putting the collage together. When a suggestion is offered, avoid a long discussion and encourage the class to try it out. This is how we best discover whether ideas work or not.

If possible record the experiments. It is easier to judge what works when we are not engrossed in performing.

◻ **If possible watch Music Explorer Programme 9**

This is a collage of musical images stimulated by Charles Ives' memories of one particular special day during his childhood. Pay particular attention to:

37–42	fragments of march-tune over slow, misty music
89–143	a collage of different march and dance tunes

Also draw attention to the way Ives *paces* his music:

47–62	after meandering until 53, the music is brought back into focus by the hymn tune and steady pulse of the basses at 54
64–74	Ives allows the music to meander again, then refocuses with the trumpet solo
81	enough meandering – time for some excitement!

Notice the *contrasts*:

43–46	a sudden burst of activity disturbs the peace
81–88	the acceleration into the marches after the stillness of the bugle-call
145	the sudden peacefulness of dawn after the noise of celebration

And the changing *density* of Ives' music:

37–46	from transparency to sudden loud busyness
74–96	from the clear solo trumpet to the many fast-moving strands of the march

The structure of Ives' 'Decoration Day' is dealt with in detail in the Music Explorer guidebook.

Project 8
Taking Turns

Preparation

The day before the lesson, ask anyone who is learning an instrument to bring it to school to use in the project.

Arrange to have the school hall or another space where the whole class can stand in a circle. Lay out a large circle of instruments and beaters, one for each pupil.

1 Count one-to-eights, alternately aloud and whispered

Start with a game. Stand in a circle with the instruments safely behind each pupil. Give a steady beat, and ask the whole class to count out loud from one to eight. Repeat, whispering. The counting never falters: aloud, whispered, aloud, whispered... Keep going.

2 Take turns to be the star

During each whispered count of one to eight, one person steps forward and performs a solo turn. It can be anything: a few steps of dance, the opening of a song, an impersonation – whatever it is, it must be short! Take turns, all the way round the circle. Nobody has time to feel foolish or vulnerable.

3 Play a solo

Sit down, take instruments and play the game again. This time each person must play a short solo during the whispered eights.

After the first circuit, suggest a variation. This time each person must play something that contrasts with the solo that went before. Fast may be followed by slow, loud by quiet, complicated by simple. Each performer must decide quickly during the one-to-eight before they perform.

A final version of the game. Each person plays what they played the previous time, but the class no longer counts nor whispers eight. Each soloist plays, then turns to the next person, who plays, and so on – a kind of musical pass-the-parcel, except that the parcel keeps changing. Can the class go right round the circle without the music stopping?

4 Develop the solo

Choose one of the solos from the circle game and show how a musical idea can be extended or *developed*. Ask the soloist to:

1 play the solo twice, repeating it exactly but changing the dynamics (loudness and quietness)

2 (for any tuned instrument) play it twice, starting the repeat one note higher so that the whole solo moves up a note

3 choose a fragment of the solo and turn it into a little piece of its own

When everyone understands these ways of

developing a piece of music, give them a little time to work on their own and develop their own solos. Then use these to perform the circle piece one last time.

⬜ If possible watch Music Explorer Programme 1
Vivaldi carries out each of the processes described in stage 4.

1–13	He repeats each phrase. First we hear it loudly, then quietly.
31–36	At 33 the violins repeat the previous shape, but starting on a higher note. Then at 35 they drop back to the same notes as at 31.
47–55	Vivaldi creates a whole section of music out of one tiny three-note fragment. 47 is repeated twice (in 48/49 and 50), starting each time one note higher. From 51 to 54 he extends the phrase by joining up more repetitions to form a *sequence* – each repetition starts one note lower.

5 Invent accompaniments for the solos

Make groups of four. Each member of the group in turn will be a soloist. The others must accompany each solo. Try to create each accompaniment out of a fragment borrowed from the solo.

Be careful that the accompaniments don't drown the soloists. Perhaps some of the accompaniments should be played by fewer than three people.

6 Compose a ritornello

When the class played the circle game, the solos were separated by 'one, two, three, four, five, six, seven, eight', out loud. Vivaldi would have called this a *ritornello*, a piece of music that returns again and again.

Ask each group to invent an instrumental ritornello – something to go between the solos and also serve as an introduction. It may borrow ideas from the solos, but it must not be too long.

7 Turn the solos, the accompaniments and the ritornello into one piece

The performers must decide which would be the most effective order for the four soloists to play so that the piece has a satisfying shape. Perhaps the most exciting solo should be kept till near the end.

Ask them to pay careful attention to dynamics. It might improve the structure of the piece if the ritornello is sometimes loud and sometimes quiet.

⬜ Watch Programme 1 again. How has this piece been put together?
Look at the diagram of Vivaldi's structure on page 7 of the *Music Explorer* guidebook. The most exciting section, the storm, comes in the second half, leaving just the right amount of time to relax into the ending. Notice also:
- when the ritornello is loud and when it is quiet
- how the soloist plays sometimes alone and sometimes as part of the orchestra

In this case there is no taking of turns; Vivaldi's piece is a solo concerto, and the violinist gets all the solos. Most concertos, like this one, have one soloist. However, others, like Bach's Brandenburg Concerto No 2 (Programme 2) have more than one soloist, and occasionally a composer writes a concerto in which many members of the orchestra take turns as soloists (Bartók: Programme 11).

Project 9
Shaping the Tune

This project is a little different from the others – it is ideally done individually, at a keyboard. It can be photocopied, and the instructions followed in detail by each individual. However, working in pairs is also quite possible.

The project is about how to mould a melody – like shaping clay. It focuses on stretching upwards and then relaxing to a 'home' note, a position of rest.

1 Invent a shapely phrase

If you are working on an electronic keyboard, select a sound that will sustain notes (organ, flute, clarinet, for example). Hold a low C with your left hand. This note will accompany the first section of melody you invent.

With your right hand, invent a short, shapely phrase about twelve notes long. Let it start on E and revolve round that note, sometimes going above it and sometimes below, finishing on D. Try to use only the five notes labelled in the diagram, together with the low C in the left hand:

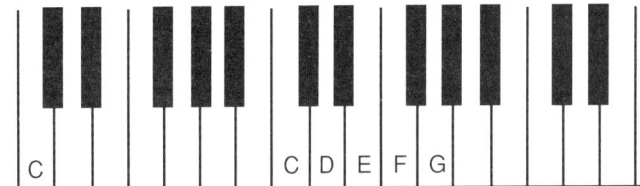

2 Invent an answering phrase

Still with C in the left hand, and still using the same block of notes, invent a second phrase, starting the same as the first but finishing on C instead of D. This answering phrase is a way of making your first phrase into a longer tune. It should feel like an extension of the first phrase.

3 Invent another pair of phrases using higher notes

Move your left hand to the F above the low C you have been playing.

Similarly, move your right hand to cover the five notes starting with F – four notes higher than before:

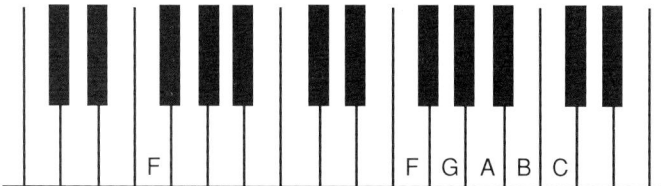

Now invent another pair of expressive phrases, similar in character to the first two but using this new set of notes. Start on high A. You decide on which note each phrase should end.

4 Round off the tune

To do this, return your left hand to C. This is the 'home' note (the *tonic*), and will help to bring the melody home – to give it a sense of conclusion.

Now, with the right hand, make a last pair of phrases to round off the whole tune. They can start exactly as the very first phrase started, but this time they need not be restricted to five notes – the last phrase can rise so that it reaches the highest note of all. This is the climax of the tune. Then make your tune relax and finish.

If you want the left hand to return briefly to F towards the end of these two phrases, you may do so. But try to finish with both hands playing Cs.

When you are satisfied with your tune, watch Music Explorer Programme 6 and listen to Dvořák's cor anglais melody, from 7 to 18

His melody has a similar structure to yours. His first two phrases (7 to 10) revolve around the first note, sometimes going above, sometimes below. His third phrase (11 to 12) has a similar (but not the same) shape, and a similar character – the tune continues to move smoothly and calmly. Dvořák lengthens this section of tune by repeating it exactly (13 to 14).

The next phrase (15 to 16) is identical to the beginning, but the answering phrase (17) soars to the highest note of all before settling back onto a satisfying final note (18).

To finish, the clarinet takes over and plays the last five notes twice – first at the same speed as the cor anglais (19), then twice as slowly (20).

Project 10

Perform this Graphic Score

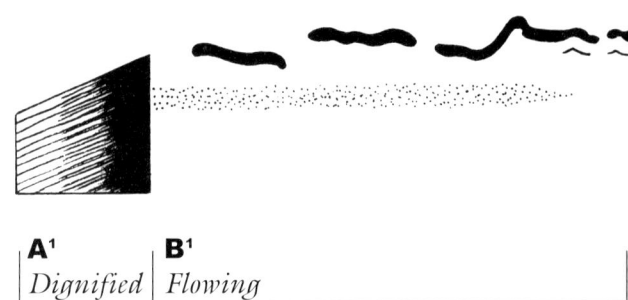

A¹ | **B¹**
Dignified | *Flowing*

This can be photocopied, and participants can work directly from the printed instructions, inventing and developing their own ideas in groups, without teacher input.

1 Look at the score (above). Then look through the instructions. Imagine the sort of music you will want to invent

The diagram is a *graphic score* – a visual map of a piece of music.

Your job is to turn the score into music. Read quickly through the rest of the project. Try to imagine the sort of music you will invent to bring this score to life – leave the exact details until later – then plan which instruments you will need, and in what order you will do the project.

2 Invent music for sections A¹ and A²

These large blocks are marked 'Dignified'. They represent blocks of strong, serious music that stand like two stone pillars on either side of section B¹.

As you read from left to right, the blocks become darker. Invent music that builds up.

The two blocks are similar but not identical. Use different instruments the

second time. What changes of instrument will you make?

3 Invent music for section B¹

This is marked 'Flowing'. The line represents a very slow, gentle, dreamlike melody played by a solo instrument. Make it dreamy both in its quietness and in the way it repeats itself, seeming in no hurry to go anywhere.

It is accompanied by a background of soft sound.

Invent also a link from B¹ to A² – a short, graceful rising phrase, like the shape on the score.

4 Invent music for section C

This is marked 'Dreamlike', and should be a development of section B¹. Use the same musical ingredients, but not just one solo instrument. Musical shapes from B¹ are woven together to make a soft texture in which all instruments sound equal.

Section C glides smoothly into section B².

5 Invent music for section B²

Begin exactly the same as section B¹ and use the same solo melody. Look closely at the line that represents the melody. It is intended

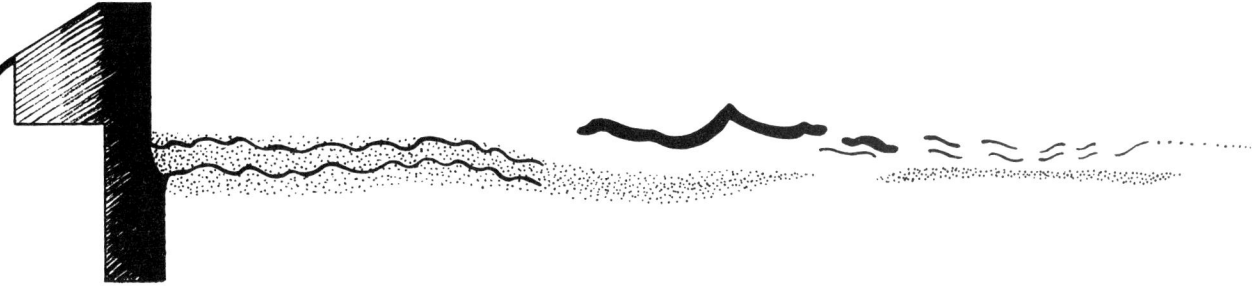

A²	**C**		**B²**		**Extension**
Dignified	*Dreamlike*		*Flowing*		*Fading away*

to show the music building up to a strong climax.

6 Invent music for the extension

This continues from, and extends, section B², gradually fading away. Find a way of winding down from the climax and finishing the piece very quietly and peacefully.

☐ **When you have completed and performed your piece, watch Music Explorer Programme 6**

This is the music that the graphic score is trying to show. Follow the score as you listen. Do you think the graphic score is an adequate diagram of the music on the video or could you think of ways to improve it?

Do you feel that this shape works well as a piece of music or would you have preferred it if Dvořák had arranged the sections in a different order?

Do you like the instruments Dvořák chose for his music? Can you imagine how the music would have sounded if he had chosen, for example:

- string instruments to play the opening music
- a trumpet to play the solo from 7
- wind instruments to play from 26 to 35
- a bassoon to play the melody when it returns at 36
- flutes to play the ending from 42

Project 11
Shadow Dances

Preparation
The first part of this project needs plenty of space for participants to move around.

1 Mime different emotions
Think about the way we use gestures to convey our feelings. Ask someone to imagine they have just received a letter containing special news. Can they perform a short mime to show how they feel? The class can try to guess what sort of news the letter contains.

Invite someone else to mime a different emotion.

2 Turn the mime into a dance
Help everyone to understand the difference between mime and dance. Whereas mime silently mimics life, dance is freer, more expressive, and perhaps more rhythmical.

Ask one of the mime performers to transform their mime into a short dance – nothing complicated, a few steps and gestures will do.

3 Add a shadow to the dance
Working in pairs, one person invents a few dance movements expressing one emotion. Can the other person shadow every move the dancer makes, so that the two dance in perfect unison? Perhaps they should dance facing one another, as if looking in a mirror. Give each pair the chance to perform.

4 Invent a tune for the shadow dance
Ask one of the dancing pairs to perform again. While they dance, ask the class to think about the sort of tune that would be appropriate to their movements. Are they smooth, jerky, fast, slow, energetic, calm?

Can somebody take a tuned instrument (a xylophone, a metallophone, a violin, a recorder, perhaps) and make up a short tune that captures the mood of the dancers' movements?

5 Add a shadow to the tune
When the tune is ready, ask someone to partner the musician and create a shadow to the tune, in a similar way to the second dancer shadowing the first dancer's every move.

However, this is not easy to do accurately. The second musician must decide which note to start on, then move note for note parallel to the tune, going higher when the tune goes higher, leaping the same number of notes when the tune leaps, etc. For example:

if player 1 plays   E F G F E
player 2 might play C D E D C

The melodic contour will always be the

same, and the two players must start together, and stay synchronised.

Ask player 2 to try shadowing on adjacent notes (e.g. D E F E D with player 1's E F G F E). We call this playing *in seconds*. People may find the effect quite strident. How does it sound if the shadow starts one note further away from the tune – *in thirds*? The effect is quite different. Can anyone find words to describe the difference?

□ **If possible watch Music Explorer Programme 11, from the beginning to 24. Can you see the connection?**
Bartók's second bassoonist shadows his colleague in exactly this way. Every note is matched exactly. The bassoonists play in sixths.

6 Match shadow tunes to shadow dances

When everyone understands how to create shadow tunes, divide into groups of four. The two musicians in each group must invent a tune for the other two's shadow dance, then they must learn to play it as a shadow tune – in seconds, thirds, fourths, fifths, sixths or sevenths. Each interval has its own distinctive character; the group must decide which is most effective for their tune and their dance.

When this task is completed, ask dancers and musicians to swap over, so that everyone has a chance to be both dancer and musician.

7 Invent accompaniments for the shadow tunes

If the music has worked well, suggest that each group turns its shadow tune into a piece of music *without* dance. Ask two members of the group to use instruments (or their voices) to invent an accompaniment for

the other pair's shadow tune.

Finally, they might invent a short introduction, and a brief linking section that allows the tune players and accompanists to swap over, so that all the music they have invented can be performed as one continuous piece. They might even finish with a special ending, a *coda*, to balance the introduction.

□ **Watch Programme 11 again, this time as far as 122. Can you hear more shadow tunes?**
At 25 the oboes play in thirds, then at 45 the clarinets take over in sevenths. The flutes play in fifths (60 to 86) and the trumpets conclude the first section of the movement playing in seconds (from 90).

Point out how imaginatively Bartók accompanies his parallel tunes, particularly the mysterious washes of string and harp colour that accompany the trumpets. And notice the introduction (1 to 8) and the little linking passages between tunes (at 41, 57 and 87). Bartók rounds off this section of the piece by returning to the music of the introduction, at 120.

The structure of the complete movement is explained in the Music Explorer guidebook.

Project 12
Disruptive Behaviour

Preparation

Set out glockenspiels, xylophones, metallophones. Replace all Bs with Bbs. Lay out also a small selection of untuned instruments for each group (claves, woodblocks, triangles – nothing too heavy-sounding).

1 Learn to play this bit of march-tune:

Play the first note, the D, as an *upbeat* – a light, preparatory note – so that the first strong beat falls on the E. The E, F and A should be strong and detached, marking the beat of the march.

In notation it looks like this:

2 Invent a lively march, starting with the bit you have learned. Invent an accompaniment for your march

Divide the class into an even number of groups and ask each group to invent a lively march-tune starting with the fragment above.

If one member of the group plays the opening phrase, another could provide an answering one.

Accompany the tune with a drone – a repeated low D. The remaining members of the group add a light rhythmical accompaniment using the untuned percussion instruments.

3 Add another layer of tune

Make a second tune that fits well when played at the same time as the march-tune. It can start later, and with the same notes as the march – like a round – and it can be just a few notes long. The objective is to get the feeling of another melodic layer – something else happening.

4 Pair up the groups and make a longer musical structure, in A B A form

When the music is ready, ask each double group to organise their music into an A B A form, for example:

Group 1 - Group 2 - Group 1

This is the music which, in stages 5 and 6, will be subject to the 'disruptive behaviour' of the project's title!

5 Invent bullying interruptions

Now give group 1 and group 2 in each double group separate tasks.

Group 1 should invent an aggressive musical interruption which will be used to attack group 2's march, like a bully picking on someone. This too should begin with the same three notes as the march, D E F, but played ferociously, and accompanied with as much loud percussion as they wish. They must decide whether the interruption is to be short or long (they can add more notes if they wish), and whether or not it should remain loud throughout.

Group 2 should invent an interruption in a military style, to attack group 1's march.

Visit each group as they work, and make sure that they understand that the interruptions are only ingredients that will be used to disrupt the march music. They are not complete pieces of music.

6 Put the marches and interruptions together

Each double group now has four ingredients: two marches and two interruptions. Ask them now to put this material together.

First the task must be discussed, deciding at what point group 2 should interrupt group 1's march and trying to imagine what it will sound like. Next, give each group a chance to try it out in front of the class so that everyone can learn from each group's ideas. Did it sound as they expected?

Then group 1 takes over the interrupting role.

After trying out the interruptions each double group must map out a structure so that the piece runs from beginning to end without stopping. Should one group give way when the other interrupts or not?

If possible record these first efforts. With several different layers and elements the music is becoming quite complex, and the performers will find it easier to judge the effectiveness of their creations when they are not involved in performing. If the performance sounds jumbled, ask them to find a way of making it sound clearer. Perhaps everyone is playing loudly in an effort to be heard. The piece will be transformed if the marches remain quiet throughout.

7 Add an introduction and an ending

Just as a carefully chosen picture-frame can set off a painting, an introduction and a *coda* (a special ending) can enhance a piece of music. Perhaps the introduction should set the mood and the coda should bring it to a strong or possibly a mysterious end.

If possible watch Music Explorer Programme 5 from 504

This almost motionless music is Mahler's introduction, a way of lulling us into a false sense of security. For suddenly, at 519, the violas shatter the stillness. Can the class see the connection with the project they have just completed? Their interruptions, like Mahler's, use the first three notes of the march-tune. Gradually the violas become calmer, dying away before Mahler's march begins.

532   The violins begin Mahler's march using the same musical shape as the project march.

533   They are immediately imitated by a cello counter-melody.

540   The aggressive violas interrupt with a developed version of 519. The three notes have become a long phrase.

557–558 A second interruption is heard, a distant fanfare of horns.

560   The violas snarl one last time.

Project 13

Decoration Day

Imagine a small American town, about 100 years ago. It's an annual holiday called 'Decoration Day' – a memorial to those who died during the War of Independence. A young boy sits on a wall, watching the events of the day. Later, he remembers the day, like a dream. This is what he remembers:

- **Through the morning mist, people making preparations. Musical instruments being practised. Bells ringing in the distance.**
- **In the old wooden church, a solemn hymn, followed by a slow, sad bugle call played by a solitary bugler.**
- **Then excitement and rejoicing. Marching bands. Old and young alike celebrating until dawn breaks.**

Picture the scene. Imagine what it was like. Paint a musical picture of the day. Start by working on the third thing the boy later remembered – the marching bands.

1 Invent a march rhythm

Ask somebody to march briskly across the room, and then to continue marching on the spot, feet beating out the steady pulse of the march. Everyone can call out with the beat: 'left, right, left, right...'.

Invite someone to add a drum-beat to the pulse of the marcher's feet. Someone else can choose another percussion instrument and add another rhythmic part.

Encourage those who choose the bigger, louder instruments to play less often than the others. For example, a large drum might play only every other beat (on each 'left', say), whereas claves might play a faster rhythm pattern – though still fitting with the march beat.

Divide into groups and ask each group to invent the rhythms of a march. Ask them to practise quietly, using only body sounds, but imagining how it will sound when they use real instruments.

Then allow each group to perform using instruments. Was the result what they expected? What alterations would they like to make, now that they have heard it on instruments?

2 Invent a march-tune

While someone plays the beat of the march, ask someone else to invent the first short phrase of a march-tune. Then someone else can invent an answering phrase.

When everyone understands what is needed, go back into groups. In each group, two people should work on the tune while the rest of the group play their rhythms in accompaniment.

3 Perform all the marches, one after another, without stopping

4 Play them all together, in one great celebration

Would it create the effect of a whole town celebrating if all the groups played their marches simultaneously? Try it out.

Would it sound more or less effective if the bands arrived at the celebration one after another?

▫ **When everyone has decided how to combine the marches, watch Music Explorer Programme 9, from 89 to 143**

Listen to Charles Ives' bands celebrating Decoration Day. He manages to create the impression of several bands playing at once. Notice 'Glory, Glory Alleluia' played by clarinets with their bells up in the air at 126.

5 Create a picture of preparations heard through morning mist

Go back to the beginning of the scenario. Ask for suggestions for instruments that would sound misty. Experiment. Unlike the march, mist will not require a definite metre or rhythm.

Get back into groups to invent some morning misty music – and, through the mist, the distant sound of musicians getting their instruments ready by practising occasional fragments of their marches. Ask for this music to be as quiet and mysterious as possible.

Help the class to combine the groups to create music that is truly atmospheric. And add the distant bells. Who can find a suitable sound?

For a moment of contrast, let the music swell briefly into something louder and more energetic – and then subside again.

6 Choose a solemn hymn-tune, and a bugler

This is a serious, emotional moment for the American people. Ask the whole class very quietly to sing a hymn or some other suitably solemn tune. Can someone suggest an extra element that might be added to make it sound truly spine-tingling?

As the hymn draws to a close, a bugler plays. How should this be done? Should the 'bugle' (a different instrument could be used) be accompanied or should it play alone?

7 Run the complete scenario without stopping

- Morning mist/practising/burst of activity/bells
- Hymn-tune
- A bugler plays
- The bands strike up

Discuss any problems that arise. Those who share instruments must sit together; instruments must be picked up and put down quietly; key performers must be able to see each other.

Did the sections link together so that the music flowed from beginning to end?

8 Invent an ending

The celebrations continue 'until dawn breaks'. Should the marches die away gradually or stop suddenly? How could dawn breaking be recreated in music?

▫ **Watch Programme 9 again, this time from beginning to end**

The Music Explorer guidebook explains in detail how Ives recreated the very same scenario.

Project 14
Stretch – and Relax

Preparation

Make a photocopy of the opening tune of the second movement from Eine kleine Nachtmusik for each person.

If possible, have Music Explorer Programme 3 ready to show. (If not, use a sound recording.)

1 Stretch – and relax

Everyone should participate, slowly stretching, tensing muscles – and then equally slowly relaxing, perhaps crumpling downwards to a state of rest.

Exactly how this is done will depend on the age and inclination of the participants, and on the space available. Some will enjoy simply stretching and relaxing; for some a more structured dance-creation may be appropriate.

2 Look at the shape of Mozart's tune

Watch Programme 3 bars 1–8, or listen to the recording (see above). Ask everyone to follow the tune on their photocopies. Don't worry about whether or not they can read music; the melody is slow enough to follow note-for-note with their fingers.

- Phrase 1, despite some changes of direction, gradually works its way higher up the stave as the pitch of the notes gets higher.
- Phrase 2 is different. It starts higher still, then descends gradually. Notes are repeated, creating a lingering effect. Unlike phrase 1 there are no leaps until the very end.
- Phrase 3 is the same as phrase 1.
- Phrase 4 leaps upwards and downwards before finally settling on C, the *key-note* or *tonic*. This note has a satisfying feeling of finality.

3 Trace the shape of the music in the air

To become familiar with Mozart's tune, ask everyone to trace the shape of the melody in the air with their hands. As the melody rises, so should their hands. When it snakes around, they should find hand-movements to match.

Now clear some space and ask them to do it with the whole body. As the tune becomes familiar, ask someone to trace it from memory, listening to it in their own mind without the music playing.

4 Play Mozart's tune

Divide into small groups. For those who don't read music the note-name is written under each note (match with the note-names on xylophone/glockenspiel/metallophone bars). Suggest that one member of the group takes each phrase.

Tuned percussion instruments, like keyboards, allow the player to *see* the shape of the tune, whereas on a recorder or a violin we only *hear* the shape.

5 Feel the tune stretch and relax

Musicians often use the words 'tension' and 'relaxation'. Ask everyone to listen to Mozart's melody once more, this time with eyes closed. Can they feel the music stretch and then relax? Where do they feel this happens?

We all respond to music in individual ways, and it is difficult to gauge how someone else will be affected by a particular piece. I feel the tension increasing during phrase 1, while phrase 2 seems to relax. Phrase 4, with its wider leaps, seems quite vigorous; then at the end it relaxes onto its final note.

Ask different people to describe how they feel about this music.

6 Make a tune that stretches, then relaxes

In pairs, invent a tune with similar tensions and relaxations to Mozart's. Take turns to invent the different phrases of the tune.

- The first person's task is to invent a rising phrase that moves *in seconds* (i.e. in *steps*, to adjacent notes) and *thirds* (small leaps to next-but-one notes) and sometimes turns back on itself. Suggest that only the lowest C D E F G A on the instrument are used.

- The second person answers with a descending phrase starting on the higher C and using any of the notes below it. No leaping is allowed in this phrase.
- Phrase 3 is the same as phrase 1.
- Phrase 4 is a joint effort with some wide leaps before settling onto a note that feels final.

When the tunes are complete ask each pair to perform, sharing the phrases between them.

Return to Music Explorer Programme 3 and watch the whole movement

It is in *rondo form*, which is a little like the earlier *ritornello form*. The tune you have been exploring is the important part of the structure that returns again and again. Notice how Mozart alters the tune the last time it returns (at 81) to make the ending particularly relaxed and final.

Draw attention to the contrasting sections of music that come between the recurrences of the opening tune. These too serve to vary the tension of the music. The section from 46 to 62 is made particularly tense by the scurrying second violins and violas. The first violins and the cellos and basses seem to carry on an argument on either side.

Project 15

Power Machine

1 Perform a rhythmic chant

Start with a clapping game using the popular football rhythm:

X   X   X X X   X X X X   X X

Get the whole class to clap it, with lots of energy. Even if you don't know it, most of them will.

Then do it as a two-part round. The second part starts on the third clap:

X   X   X X X   X X X X   X X   *etc.*
　　　 X   X   X X X   X X X X   X X

Then try it in three and four parts.
Try performing it on untuned instruments: drums, claves, tambourines, etc.
Then try it on tuned instruments. On xylophones/glockenspiels/metallophones, five or six people can sit round each instrument, each playing a single note. Use

chime bars too.
Finally a continuous version. Start with clapping. Then, without stopping, transfer one at a time onto untuned percussion, then to tuned percussion, then back again, finishing with clapping. Lots of ways of using a single musical idea.

2 Invent powerful rhythmic chants

Divide into five groups. Each group must make a powerful rhythmic chant using voices and one xylophone, glockenspiel or metallophone. And each group must use a particular set of ingredients – two phrases per group, chanted on particular notes, as follows:

Group 1

A   A
'CRASH, BANG'

　　 B　C
A　　　A
'What a rac-ket'

Group 2

A B C B A
'Help! My ears will burst'

B C D A
'What a clang-ing'

Group 3

This group must use tuned percussion with F♯s and B♭s.

G F♯ G A G A B♭
'Oh! What a din, what a din'

G A B♭ C
'I can't stand it'

Group 4

A A D
'What a row'

C B B
'I'm fright-ened'

Group 5

C B A
'PLEASE stop it'

B A B C
'I'm go-ing deaf'

Use the instruments to help keep in tune.

As with the football chant, there are lots of ways of using these ingredients. For example:

- simply alternate the two fragments
- join the two fragments together to make a longer phrase and perform it as a round
- extend a fragment by repeating it as a *sequence*, starting one note higher or lower on each successive repetition
- create blocks of sound by singing the shape with each member of the group starting on a different note and moving in parallel

The words will help to find rhythms. Perhaps each group should also clap a steady pulse to make its chants sound really machine-like.

3 Combine the chants

When the chants are ready, ask each group to perform to the class. Then help everyone to assemble a single piece out of all the chants. They might start by choosing an order and performing the chants one after another without stopping. Then they might try some overlapping.

4 Punctuate the music with a drum

When the class has experimented a little, add another ingredient. Ask them to punctuate the music with a drum, perhaps using it to signal where one group finishes and another begins.

5 Build up to a climax

Ask the class to compress their music and make it as dense as possible. They must decide:

- whether still to perform their chants one after the other, or whether to overlap them
- how to build up and create a climax to the piece

- whether they would like to add more instruments

6 Add dynamics

Ask the class to think carefully about how they might use *dynamics* – loud and quiet, getting louder (*crescendo*) and getting quieter (*diminuendo*) – to add to the effectiveness of their music.

If possible watch Music Explorer Programme 12. Can you see the connections?

Shostakovich's music is a portrait of the Russian dictator Joseph Stalin, one of the most terrifying power machines the world has ever known. Each group's musical ingredients are borrowed from Shostakovich's music. Play the movement and help the groups to identify their fragment:

1–6	group 1
7–10	group 2
21–22	group 3
67–69	group 4
181–184	group 5

Then help them to see how Shostakovich builds a movement out of the ingredients. The structure is explained in the *Music Explorer* guidebook.

Group 1's material is perhaps the most important. It returns again and again as a structural landmark.

Shostakovich generally uses his ingredients one at a time. But at 213, as the movement approaches its climax, group 1 and group 2 (played in slow motion on the bass instruments, then later, at 243, on wind, trumpets and horns) are combined.

Shostakovich, too, punctuates his music with a drum – a snare drum (at 31, 66, 70, 73, 76, 86, 98, 97, etc.).

Project 16
Fives

1 Count fives

Count out a steady beat, at about two beats a second. Count fives (count up to 5, then start again at 1, continuously).

1 2 3 4 5 1 2 3 4 5 *etc.*

Ask everyone to clap each time you say 'One':

1 2 3 4 5 1 2 3 4 5
x   **x**   *etc.*

2 Invent a rhythm that fits the fives

Ask someone to invent a rhythm that fits into the five beats. Everyone else continues to clap on beat 1. For example:

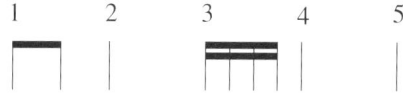

Ask for the rhythm to be repeated several times, so that everyone can learn it. Then take over the clapping so that the whole class can join in with the rhythm.

Perhaps add words to fit the rhythm. This will help to memorise it.

3 Invent new rhythms

Still using the cycle of five beats, play the game several times inviting different volunteers to invent new rhythms.

4 Play clap-and-answer in a circle

Stand in a circle. While you continue to count five, clapping on beat 1, each person in turn invents a rhythm and the rest of the class immediately claps it back. Move swiftly round the circle, encouraging each attempt, so that nobody has time to fail or feel foolish.

5 Invent a powerful five-beat rhythm

Now that everybody understands how to fit a rhythm into five beats, divide into groups and ask each group to invent a powerful, driving rhythm in five beats to the bar.

Ask each group to perform its rhythm to the class. If the rhythms feel secure, try getting several groups (or all of them) to perform simultaneously.

When the beat is in a cycle of five, we say that the music has 'five beats to the bar' or is 'in five'.

6 Use instruments to play the rhythms

Ask each group to *orchestrate* its rhythm, using percussion instruments. Different instruments could play different parts of the rhythm – but ask one member of the group to play the complete rhythm, using the note C, e.g. on xylophone or chime bar.

If possible watch Music Explorer Programme 10, from the beginning to 40. Can you see the connections?

Holst's rhythm is also in five. At the beginning we see it played with the wooden part of a cello bow (*col legno*), by a harp, then by a violin bow.

Holst uses other instruments to play short fragments of tune. The first fragment comes almost immediately, at 3 (bassoons). Ask the class to tell you when the second comes in [at 8 on contrabassoon].

7 Add short layers of tune over the rhythm

Ask one of the groups to play its rhythm very quietly to the class. Can someone from another group invent a fragment of tune and add it over the rhythm, as Holst does at 3?

Make sure each group has one or two tuned instruments so that they can add successive layers (some may wish to use their voices) until only the person playing the note C is left with the rhythm.

8 Try it all together

When all the groups have added their layers of tune, try a performance with the whole class playing at once. Since all the music revolves around the same five-beat pulse and the note C, this might work well. If not, nothing has been lost; explain that composers experiment continually to find out what works and what doesn't.

Then, instead of starting all at once, help the class to build up the music gradually. They must decide:

- which group should start, and how soon others should come in
- whether to use all the rhythms to underpin the music, or one or two only

9 Decide whether to continue or to finish

Watch Programme 10 again, but stop the video the moment it reaches 40. This is the point the class has reached with its piece. Now they must decide how to continue. They might:

- change the C to a different note, and find a way of continuing with the same or new rhythms
- find a way of 'winding down' from this point to an effective ending
- compose a contrasting middle section to their piece, perhaps by choosing one of the tune-layers they have invented and *developing* it

10 Compose a slow middle section

Ask someone to play one of the layers of tune. Then ask them to repeat it, adding one or two extra notes to make it longer. And then to repeat it again, adding more notes still.

When everyone understands this way of developing musical material, go into groups again. Each group must choose *one* of its tune fragments and develop it into a slow, smooth section of music. As a reminder that this is still the same piece of music as the rhythmic opening, ask them to accompany it with slowed-down fragments of the opening rhythm.

11 Put it all together like this: A¹ – B – A²

A² is like A¹ with an effective ending.

Watch Programme 10 again, this time all the way through

Can everyone make a connection between the way Holst constructs his middle section (96–110) and the way they constructed theirs?

How exciting it is when Holst crashes back into his opening music at 110!

Project 17
Aggressive Gestures

1 Circle clapping game with names

Stand in a circle. Everyone claps, counting a cycle of eight beats. On beats 5 and 6 the claps are silent, and each person in turn chants their name, like this:

    x   x   x   x   x   x   x   x
    clap clap clap clap Fati-ma *clap clap*
    clap clap clap clap Mar-tin *clap clap*
    etc.

Next, make beats 7 and 8 silent. Mime the silent claps, so that everyone can feel the continuous pulse:

    clap clap clap clap Fati-ma [*clap clap*]

Play the game again – but this time everyone repeats each name during the last two silent claps:

            (solo:)   *(all:)*
  clap clap clap clap Fati-ma FATI-MA

2 Do the same, but with aggressive gestures in place of the names

Not rude gestures, please, but strong, simple, dramatic poses or simple movements.

Go through the same sequence of stages. Finally, individuals in turn make their gestures on beats 5 and 6, with everyone imitating on 7 and 8.

3 Convert the aggressive gestures to musical gestures

Place a tuned percussion instrument in the middle of the circle, with the notes set up as described above. Demonstrate an aggressive musical gesture – as brief as the physical gestures of stage 2, but played on the instrument. You could play almost anything, but it should be brief, distinctive, memorable.

When everyone understands what is meant by 'musical gesture', go into groups of six, each group around a xylophone, glockenspiel or metallophone, and invent a circle of musical gestures. Those who learn instruments may prefer to use their own instrument when their turn comes. Each player must invent something they can play the same every time.

4 Add a rapid G drone

When the gestures are ready, drop the clapping, and ask each group to choose someone to add a rapidly repeated G, played with two beaters. This drone will accompany the gestures and drive the music forward.

When the drone-player's turn comes to play a gesture, someone else must take over the drone.

5 Add an accompaniment to each gesture

When the groups have rehearsed their gestures with the rapid G drone, add another ingredient. Ask each player to take another percussion instrument and, choosing a partner, accompany the partner's gesture when its turn comes.

All this activity will test the group's organisation. Give them time to rehearse until their performance is really efficient.

◻ If possible watch Music Explorer Programme 8, as far as 37. Can you see connections?

In the Russian legend of The Firebird, King Kastchei is an evil magician who turns people into stone. He bursts out of his haunted castle and performs a terrifying dance.

Stravinsky builds the entire opening section of the dance out of two aggressive gestures, the first on bassoons and horns at 3 and 4, and the second on trombones at 9 and 10. A continuous drone note is played by the timpani.

6 Turn the gesture music into an 'Infernal Dance', with loud bangs added

Give the groups a little more freedom. Keep the drone, but instead of playing one after another in order round the circle, allow the players to use the ingredients more freely to create a structure that really works. For instance, they could:

- repeat some gestures, perhaps keeping the same shape but starting on a different note
- add extra notes to make some gestures

longer (*develop* them)
- play two gestures simultaneously

To punctuate the music, add sudden bangs played by everybody at once.

7 Invent a contrasting section of music

Contrast is an important tool in the hands of a good composer. To make a contrast here, invent a smooth tune, still in the same mode. Make it smooth by moving mostly to adjacent notes. A change of instrument may be desirable; it is difficult to make smooth tunes on a xylophone!

Accompany the tune with a simple ostinato. Then, when the ostinato is ready, invite the other members of the group to fill out the accompaniment using untuned instruments or notes from the mode.

8 Put the whole dance together

Suggest that each group try alternating aggressive gestures and smooth tune. Encourage them to make the music flow from beginning to end without any awkward gaps.

◻ Watch Programme 8 again, this time right through. Can you see more connections?

39   Stravinsky's first contrasting section, a smooth tune played by violins and accompanied by an ostinato (second violins and violas)

55   back to the aggressive gesture music

99   a second smooth tune

143   the gesture music again – this structure, repeatedly returning to the opening music, is called *rondo form*

177   Stravinsky abandons rondo form and storms through to the end of the dance in a blaze of orchestral virtuosity

Project 18
Musical Tennis

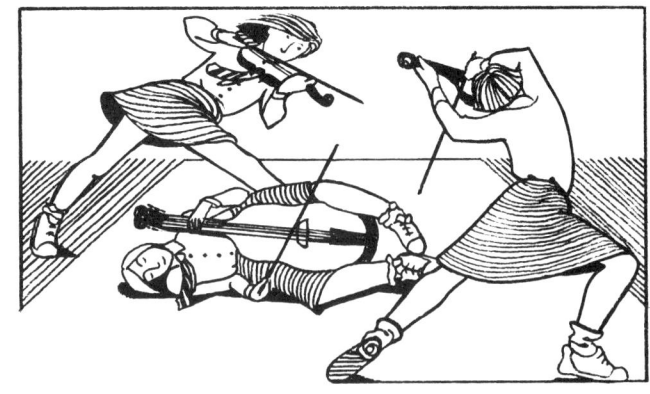

Preparation

Put out as many xylophones, glockenspiels and metallophones as possible. Each group of three people will need at least one instrument. Encourage any pupils who learn instruments to use them.

1 Invent a word-game for two players and commentator

The two players should bat words or short phrases back and forth, alternating. The third person provides a continuous commentary – not too loud, so that the two players can be clearly heard; yet the commentary, too, should be audible.

On what would people like to base the word-game? Here are some suggestions:

1   Tennis. The players alternately describe their strokes: 'Serve down the centre' - 'backhand return' - 'forehand volley' - 'backhand drive' and so on. Meanwhile the commentary murmurs on: 'And she comes forward to the net, putting the pressure on' etc.

2   Football. Each player represents a team: 'Cantona kicks off' - 'Gascoigne closes him down' - 'He slips it sideways to Giggs' etc. Again with commentary.

3   An argument – but it musn't get too heated. It could be Question Time in the House of Commons, with the players acting the two opposing politicians, plus a quiet commentary. Or a domestic argument.

4   Shop counter. 'Two choc ices please' - 'one pound please' etc., again with commentary.

All this may cause some amusement, but there's a serious objective. Encourage groups to look beyond the word-meanings and make an effective web of sound, where two partners or protagonists are trading phrases across a continuous background of sound.

2 Turn the commentary into a musical strand

In the word-game the players play back and forth across the commentary – as if it were the tennis net, or the shop counter. Now make this continuous strand into a line of music. Using a xylophone, glockenspiel or metallophone, with two beaters, ask someone to invent a line of music that moves always *in parallel thirds*. This means that whatever the right hand plays, the left hand must duplicate two notes away.

Suggest that the music should snake along, moving mostly to adjacent notes. Ask the player to invent something that can easily be remembered, so that it can be repeated accurately.

When the task is clearly understood, go back into threes to invent the line of thirds. The group must agree on something they like, then decide who will perform it.

3 Turn the players' phrases into music. Make the phrases imitate each other

These are like the shots the tennis stars make: first one, then the other. Think about it first. One person must play or sing a musical shape – three notes will do. Then the other must play the shape back, perhaps the same or perhaps in a different version.

For example, the shape might come back at a different pitch – perhaps an octave higher or lower – or upside down or backwards, or extended with extra notes.

Choose instruments and experiment. Encourage the players to develop the shape progressively, so that the different versions arise gradually.

Perhaps the commentator should umpire and decide which version works best!

4 Send the shapes across the line of thirds

Now is the time for all three members of the group to perform together. As the line of thirds and the shape were invented separately, they may not work well together. Try them, then decide what modifications are needed to make a satisfying piece of music.

If possible watch Music Explorer Programme 3 from 46. Can you see the connections?

Watch for the violas at 46, 50–51, 54 and 61. They always play in thirds with the second violins and they move mostly to adjacent notes. You can hear them playing continuously during the whole of this section of the movement. Point out how Mozart increases the tension of the line by repeating each note. At 54 and 61 you can clearly see the bows bounce twice before the fingers move to the next note.

This continuous line of music is important. It binds the music together and carries it forward. Without it the musical shapes that bounce back and forth between first violins and cellos and basses would seem disembodied and meaningless.

At 47 the cellos and basses imitate the first violins, playing the same shape.

At 49 they come together to finish the first phrase.

At 54 there is more imitation, then at 57 the violins develop the shape into a string of notes and are imitated by the cellos and basses in 58.

59 is the climax of the section. The cellos and basses crowd the violins, still imitating but almost on top of them, before Mozart relaxes into the return of less urgent music.

When you have explored the imitations, watch the whole of Programme 3 and notice what an effective contrast this middle section makes to the rest of the movement.

Project 19
Sequences and Signatures

1 Play some echo games

Clap a rhythm and ask everyone to clap it back to you immediately, like an echo. Clap another, and another. Ask someone to take your place, then someone else.

Take over again and say a short phrase; anything will do. Again everyone must echo you. Now sing a short musical phrase. Again an echo.

Divide into groups of about eight, and let them play the game sitting in circles. The first person sings a phrase and the group echoes it. Again the soloist sings the phrase and again the group responds. Then the solo role passes to the next person in the circle, who invents a new phrase.

Finally, ask each group to choose one of their phrases and to sing it all together. The group will use this as their 'musical signature' later in the project. The rest of the class must echo it loudly.

2 Sing some sequences

Play a variation of the last game, using sequences. Sing a simple phrase in a deep voice. The group echoes. Then sing the same phrase starting one note higher; the group echoes; and so on. Then try a sequence that starts high and goes lower.

Go back into groups to play this new game. If they find it difficult, suggest that they use a xylophone, a glockenspiel or a metallophone as well as singing. The first person plays a phrase on the instrument; the group sings it back. The second person takes over at the instrument and plays the same shape one note higher; the group sings it; and so on.

If possible watch Music Explorer Programme 4, from 398 to 479. Can you see any connections?

After the first flurry of notes, Beethoven starts a sequence. Point out the cellist playing the sequence from 407 to 414. And at 423 the violins start another sequence.

Watch the flutes at 439. They play a tiny phrase which is immediately echoed by the violins (443). Let the video play on. Which other echoes can the class pick out?

Although Beethoven wrote some wonderful melodies, much of his music contains no melody at all. He had a genius for using small phrases to build great spans of music, like an architect designing a bridge.

3 Combine a drone with a sequence

Go back into groups and ask each group to choose an instrument that can sustain a long note: a keyboard, a wind or string instrument, or a continuously repeated note on a metallophone. Give each group a different drone note – low C, low D, low F and low G – and ask them each to invent a new sequence-piece over their drone.

As a starting point, suggest that the sequence start on the same note as the drone. For example:

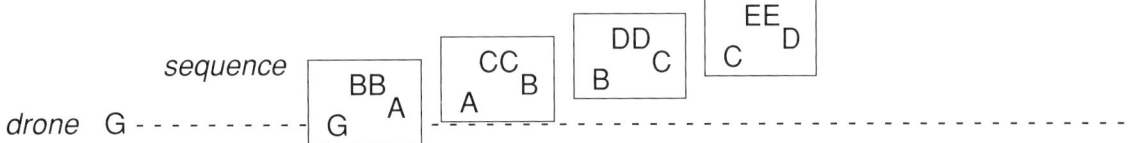

When they understand how this works, some groups may wish to choose a starting-note that is different from their drone-note.

4 Put together a piece combining drones, sequences and signatures

Remind everyone of the musical ingredients they have assembled. Each group has two: a sequence piece accompanied by a drone, and a musical signature, sung by the whole group and echoed by the rest of the class. Ask each group to perform its two ingredients once more.

Then help the class to use these ingredients to make one complete drones, sequences and signatures piece.

Watch Programme 4 again, this time from the beginning to 122

Beethoven's 'signature' is the powerful four-note phrase that starts the symphony, played by the whole orchestra in unison. Notice how most of the music that comes before the smooth tune at 63 is constructed from this phrase. Notice too how the tune is echoed first by the clarinet at 67, then by the flute at 71. Echoes play an important part in the construction of this movement. Encourage the class to listen for them.

Draw attention to the violin sequence that starts at 38. Then watch the complete movement, pointing out other sequences starting at 158 and 282 as you reach them.

Project 20
Grand Bathing Ceremony

Preparation

Set out glockenspiels, xylophones, metallophones. Remove all the E and B bars, leaving C D F G A. Have soft beaters ready for stage 1, hard beaters for stage 2.

Also provide quiet untuned percussion – not cymbals or drums at first, though cymbals may be useful for stage 6, and both for stage 8.

1 Make a mysterious shimmer of sound

Demonstrate this idea with four volunteers round a xylophone (two on each side). They must quickly decide whether to play all together or not, and whether to play to a beat or to play freely.

Then divide into an even number of groups. Give each group a xylophone, metallophone or glockenspiel, plus beaters, and ask each group to make its own shimmer. Suitable untuned instruments can be added (Indian bells or triangles might be effective) if they wish.

This shimmer is to be the accompaniment to the first tune in our pieces.

2 Make a lively march-like tune

Ask each group to invent one – it can be very short. It can be played on any instrument(s), but must use the same C D F G A (*pentatonic*) scale as the shimmering music. Ask that it be shared between two people, the first inventing a short phrase and the second answering it with another.

3 Put the tune and the shimmer together

Each group should find a way of combining its tune with the shimmering accompaniment.

Give each group a chance to play for the class. Can the tunes be heard clearly over the accompaniments? If not, how can this problem be solved? Perhaps the tune needs to be louder or the accompaniment softer.

4 Combine two groups in succession

Pairs of groups join up, playing their tunes and shimmering backgrounds one after the other, with a smooth 'join' from one group to the other. Perhaps overlap or combine the shimmers.

5 Add an introduction

Next, ask each of these double groups to work out an introduction, so forming this sequence:

    introduction - tune A - tune B

The introduction could be based on the shimmering effects or it could be something different. But it shouldn't steal the thunder from the first tune; it should be a preparation.

6 Add two momentary splashes of sound

This is like adding spice to a mixture. The splashes can come any time during tune A or tune B. They should involve all or most of the players.

If possible watch Music Explorer Programme 7, from 1 to 68. Can you see the connections?

1–9	introduction
9–31	first tune
32–55	second tune
24–29	splashes of sound

Ravel headed his piece with this text:
  Laideronnette: Empress of the Pagodas
  She undressed and got into the bath. Soon elves
  and pixies began to sing and to play
  instruments; some had lutes made of walnut
  shells; some had viols made of almond shells; for
  their instruments were well suited to their size.
This may draw laughter – perhaps the splashes of
sound represent the Empress dropping the soap into
the bath! – but the description is intended to suggest
a ritual, a ceremonial bathing with all the
attendant mystery of a special occasion. The next
stage in the music will reflect this, by being more
stately and serious.

7 Invent a slow, dignified tune

Keep in the double-sized groups, and keep using the same pentatonic scale. The new tune should contrast with the two lively tunes. When the groups have worked out the notes they want, suggest that the tune will sound more weighty if it is performed by several players at once – using different instruments, or at different octaves, or perhaps using voices, depending on what is available.

Can the remaining players find a way of punctuating the tune using appropriately important and oriental-sounding percussion?

As an optional refinement, could the players repeat the dignified tune as a round (*in canon*)? (With pentatonic tunes everything tends to fit with everything else, so that shouldn't be a problem.)

8 Put the whole thing together like this: introduction - two lively tunes - dignified tune - the lively tunes again - ending

Explain that the dignified tune will be a contrasting middle section, followed by a return to the lively tunes. The groups must find a way of linking all the sections together so that the piece runs continuously.

What would make a really effective ending?

Watch Programme 7 again, this time right through. Can you see more connections?

69–82	Ravel sets up the slower tempo
83	The dignified tune, played by a clarinet and punctuated by the gong
93	A canon between celeste (which starts at 93) and clarinet (which re-starts at 95)
142	Return of the lively tunes

The structure is clearly explained in the Music Explorer guidebook, and many more details in the music and the performance are examined.

Project 21
Miniature Jigsaws

This project is quite challenging, for pupils working in pairs, using tuned instruments. It can be photo-copied and given to the pairs to work on their own.

Those who are learning an instrument should use their own instrument if possible. Others should work with tuned percussion or keyboards – two at one instrument if necessary.

The project is linked to Programme 8 on the Music Explorer video, but also makes reference to two other relevant programmes.

1 Invent a short musical shape, about seven notes long

This is like a single piece of a jigsaw. When you are satisfied with your shape, ask your partner to play exactly the same shape, but starting on a different note. Your partner must make exactly the same moves as you made in your shape.

Play one after the other. Then try overlapping the two statements of the shape, the second player starting just before the first finishes.

Experiment a bit more. Try starting the overlapping answering shape on different notes. If the second player started on C last time, try starting on D this time, for example. Keep trying until you find something that really works well. Practise it until you can play it perfectly.

2 Change round so that player 2 plays first

It's player 2's turn to invent a shape. And player 1's turn to learn it, then to overlap it.

What you have invented is the beginning of a piece of contrapuntal music for two players. In much music, one part (the tune, for example) is more prominent than the other part (the accompaniment). The word 'contrapuntal' describes music in which each part is equally interesting and equally important. It means 'part against part', with the parts fitting neatly together like a jigsaw.

If possible watch Music Explorer Programme 2 from the beginning

This is by far the most contrapuntal piece of music on the video. Here every solo part is of equal importance and interest. Notice the difference between the solo instruments' contrapuntal music and the accompanying role taken by the strings at 47.

3 Find a way of continuing the piece

Play straight through what you have invented so far without stopping. Then repeat it so that the audience will have a chance to appreciate it. Now continue your piece, making sure that both parts are equally interesting to play. You might:

- continue the overlapping idea – but not for too long, as all music needs a change after a while
- invent a more continuous section of music in which you take quickly-changing turns to move, just three or four notes each at a time
- move along together for a while, either in *similar motion* (the same direction up or down in pitch)

or in *contrary motion* (opposite directions)

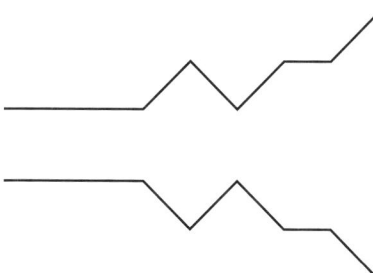

Now look at Music Explorer Programme 11

Bartók provides a superb example of similar motion. All the pairs of wind instruments move in similar motion. Contrary motion is harder to hear. Listen carefully from 123 to 146. The tuba moves always in the opposite direction to the tune.

4 Bring your piece to a satisfying ending

This is a miniature piece of music; it need not be long! Try bringing back some of the music you invented earlier as an ending. You may need to modify it so that it sounds really final.

When you have performed your piece, watch Programme 8, starting at 55

Stravinsky writes some wonderful contrapuntal music using two different musical shapes.

Watch first how the violin phrase at 62 is immediately imitated and overlapped by the flutes at 63. The horns play it again at 66 and the violins overlap at 67.

Then watch the trumpet at 59. The flutes overlap with the same phrase at 61. The trumpet plays again at 64, and if you listen carefully you will hear the cellos and bassoons overlap at 65 – and yet again at 68, overlapped this time by the piano at 69.

Watch the whole section again. Stravinsky is so skilful at writing counterpoint that he is able to handle both phrases in the same section of music. How dense and vibrant all this contrapuntal activity makes the music!

Project 22
Follow my Leader

1 Sing a well-known round

You might choose 'Frère Jacques', singing it first in unison, then dividing into four groups to sing it as a round.

2 Add a drone

Add an extra ingredient to the round. Ask a fifth group to sing a continuous rhythmic drone throughout the performance. They might sing:

Ding dong ding dong

Perhaps the performance should start with this group alone, singing 'Ding dong' twice before the tune enters.

Choose an effective way of ending.

3 Recite a miniature poem

I'm walking up the busy street
And pass you coming down.

Write the poem on the board and recite it together. Say 'I'm' and 'And' very lightly, so that the accent falls on 'walk-' and 'pass'.

📺 **If possible watch the opening of Music Explorer Programme 1**

Vivaldi's music starts with a similar anacrusis or *upbeat*.

Look for other upbeats at the beginning of Vivaldi's phrases. There is one at the beginning of each phrase of the ritornello (4, 7, 10).

---

4 Invent a tune for the poem

The person in the song is going *up* the street. Perhaps the music should also go up – rising in pitch for the first line. Then the other person passes on the way *down*. Suggest that the second phrase descends.

The tune must start with an upbeat, matching the words.

Pupils should work in pairs to invent a simple tune for the rhyme. They may choose either to sing the tune or to invent it on instruments. To provide a tonal centre and help singers stay in tune, suggest that one of them plays a continuously repeated drone note, for example on a low chime bar.

5 Turn the tune into a round

Divide the class into two and recite the miniature poem as a two-part round, with group 2 starting as group 1 reaches 'And'.

Now ask the pairs to try out the music they have invented as a round. If possible, record the performances. It may work or it may not. What do the performers feel about it? Would they like to alter the music to get a better fit?

In a round, the second line is a section of tune that sounds well against the music of the first line. This is called 'counterpoint', often described as 'tune against tune'.

If the second line doesn't fit very well against the first, encourage the pair to keep the first line as it is and try adjusting the music for the second line. If possible, record the first line several times in succession, and experiment by singing against the recording.

◻ **If possible watch Music Explorer Programme 2, from the beginning**
The music starts with 'Follow my leader', a bit like a round. The trumpet's music up to 7 is the first line – the equivalent of 'I'm walking up the busy street'. Then the oboe takes up the same tune, while the trumpet plays a counterpoint against it – 'And pass you coming down'.

In a real round the trumpet would then return to the beginning, and the music would go literally round and round. Bach's counterpoint is a more complex affair. This structure is called a 'fugue'; when the violin takes up the tune (or 'subject') at 21, the trumpet is given a new counterpoint to play. And so the music develops rather than repeating.

Project 23
Gossip, Gossip

Preparation
Photocopy the nonsense rhyme on the next page for each member of the class, or write it up on the board.

The underlined words show the pulse of the rhyme. It will help you and the class if you tap the pulse on your knee.

Prepare also a continuation of the rhyme for use in stage 2 of the project – your own invention, starting with 'Dead, he said...', a second verse that fits neatly with the Uncle Fred verse. It needn't be anything very clever, but it should be three lines in total, each with four beats (four stressed syllables in the manner of the first three lines).

---

1 Gossip
To demonstrate the gossip, ask two people to join you. You start the gossip:
'<u>Un</u>cle <u>Fred</u> had a <u>pain</u>...'

Un - cle   Fred   had a   pain   in   his   head   he

said,   and he   took   to   his   bed   and was   ve - ry   ve - ry

ve - ry   ve - ry   ve - ry   ve - ry   ve - ry   ve - ry   ve - ry   near-ly

DEAD,   he   said

Exactly as you reach 'DEAD', Person 2 starts:

    'Uncle Fred had a pain...'

Meanwhile you continue for just two more syllables ('he said') and then stop, making the briefest of overlaps as Person 2 picks up the rhyme. Similarly, when Person 2 reaches 'DEAD' Person 3 starts the rhyme. Person 2 stops after 'he said'.

    This first stage demonstrates the rhythm of the rhyme, and also the principle of successive entries.

2 Add another verse of gossip

Now build a full-length overlap. As before, Person 2 starts when you reach 'DEAD', but this time you don't stop after two syllables, you carry on, using your prepared continuation of the rhyme, and coordinating your stressed syllables with Person 2. For example:

...very very very nearly DEAD he said what a dread-ful   thing it...
                     Un - cle Fred had a pain   in his head he...

...and so on. You can go on to add Person 3, but in that case Person 2 will need to copy your second verse; lines 4–6 must be the same each time, just as lines 1–3 were the same each time.

    If this were a piece of music we would call it a *fugue*. The first theme or statement ('Uncle Fred...' – lines 1–3) is called the *subject*. The continuation ('DEAD, he said...' – lines 4–6) is called the *countersubject* (the music that goes 'against' the subject).

3 Make a gossip-fugue

Work in groups of four. Use lines 1–3 as they stand, but ask each group to invent their own countersubject, starting with 'DEAD, he said'. The rules are:

- Each successive person must begin as the previous person says the word 'DEAD'.
- The countersubject must use the same words every time. The groups will need to work out their countersubjects exactly and write them down.
- The countersubject must fit neatly against the words of the subject.

If possible watch Music Explorer Programme 2, from the beginning to 40. Can you see the connections?
Bach's music is a fugue. The trumpet plays the subject and then continues with the countersubject once the oboe begins at 7.

Before the next entry Bach adds some extra padding (from 15 to 20), then the violin enters (21, countersubject played by the oboe) followed by the recorder (27, countersubject played by the violin).

4 Fill in the spaces

So far the groups have performed subject and countersubject – but when Person 3 enters Person 1 drops out, having completed lines 1–6.

Now some more gossip must be invented to follow the countersubject, so that by the end all four performers are gossiping at once. Unlike the countersubject, the new words can be different for each person, but should still fit rhythmically with everything else that is going on.

Try leaving some gaps so that everyone isn't speaking all the time.

And write everything down, so that the finished fugue is the same each time it is performed, and can be made to sound really accurate and tidy.

5 Perform, with dynamics

Ask each group to perform its completed fugue. It is important in a fugue that the listeners can hear each new entry. Ask the performers to add dynamics (louds and quiets) so that the entries become clear.

Optional extension: Add sequences

If the class has enjoyed the project, borrow another of Bach's techniques and extend the fugues. Bach frequently takes a musical shape and repeats it several times starting on a succession of different notes. Such repetitions are called *sequences*. Any fragment of the rhyme, e.g. 'very nearly DEAD', could be treated in this way – repeat it several times, each time at a slightly higher or lower pitch.

In a fugue, a sequence often forms part of an *episode*, a short section when neither the subject nor the countersubject is heard in full. Ask each group to take a phrase from their fugue and use it to create an episode that contrasts with the busyness of the gossiping fugue.

Watch Programme 2 again, from 48 to 56
Bach uses episodes as a relaxation between sections of fugue. Listen to the sequences between 48 and 51. The fugue subject returns at 57, played by the violin.

Now watch Programme 2 complete

Suggest that people try saying the Uncle Fred rhyme along with the music as each player plays the subject. It should fit nicely.

Project 24
A Flying Bed

Preparation

Make eight photocopies of the short script below, or write it on the board.

1 Perform 'A Flying Bed' as a play

You are rehearsing a scene from a new play. Choose a cast of eight actors and actresses.

Only on stage would people keep saying the same words to each other like this! Has

---

Eight onlookers are on stage, gazing upwards in amazement.

ALL	A flying bed! A flying bed!
	(pause)
1st ONLOOKER	A flying bed!
2nd ONLOOKER	A flying bed?
3rd ONLOOKER	A flying bed!
	(short pause)
4th ONLOOKER	A flying bed!
5th ONLOOKER	A flying bed?
6th ONLOOKER	A flying bed!
	(short pause)
{ 7th ONLOOKER	A flying bed-----------stead? }
{ 8th ONLOOKER	It's really weird }
{ 7th ONLOOKER	A flying bed-----------stead? }
{ 8th ONLOOKER	It's really weird }
ALL	A flying bed, THAT'S WEIRD!
	(pause)
ALL	A FLYING BED!!!

anyone noticed that all of the phrases contain the same rhythm? 7th Onlooker makes it longer and 8th Onlooker interrupts with different words before 7th has finished, but the rhythm continues. It is the famous rhythm of the opening of Beethoven's Fifth Symphony: three short sounds leading to one longer or accented sound.

2 Turn it into a Musical

Ask someone to *sing* the words 'A flying bed'. Everyone sings it back in amazement, echoing the tune.

Always keeping the same musical shape, discuss how the complete script might be sung. It could sometimes start on a different note. Someone might sing it upside down. What other possibilities are there? For 'A flying bedstead' it will have to be extended by one note.

Experiment and see what works best. If pitching the notes is a problem, add instruments to help.

Now divide into groups of eight and ask each group to create its own sung version of this scene. Whatever musical phrase each group invents for the first 'A flying bed' must be the musical material for the entire scene.

3 Add dynamics and other refinements

Ask each group to perform. Have they managed to capture the sense of astonishment? Perhaps dynamics – loud and quiet (*forte* and *piano*), getting louder and getting quieter (*crescendo* and *diminuendo*) – would help. Pauses (waiting on notes or waiting in silence) might be effective.

> **If possible watch Music Explorer Programme 4, from 1 to 57. Can you see the connections?**
> Beethoven invents the entire first section of

his symphony out of this rhythm:

1–2, 3–4	played in unison
6–18	the strings play an echoing game with it
15, 17	the 2nd violins and violas play it upside down
18–21	Beethoven extends it by adding an extra note and a pause

4 Extend the scene and add instruments

Ask the groups to extend what they have invented and make a complete scene with an effective ending. They may wish to use new words, but should stick as far as possible to the same basic rhythm.

Perhaps they would like to add instruments to what they have invented.

5 Invent a contrasting section

Contrast is an important element in both music and theatre. Ask the groups to invent a contrasting section using a new section of script set to a smooth tune.

> **Watch Programme 4 again**
> Draw attention to the contrasting melody at 63. It is smooth and quiet, but lurking in the accompaniment is the 'flying bed' rhythm – almost continuous from 84.

6 Find a good way of finishing

At 94 Beethoven returns to the urgent rhythmical mood of the opening to round off the first section of the movement. Ask the groups to find their own ways of bringing their pieces to a satisfying conclusion. They might decide to emulate Beethoven or they might finish in quite a different way. Whatever they decide, it must give the audience a feeling of finality.

Music Explorer Project Book

Published by and available from
Apollo Trust,
145 Park Road, Buxton,
Derbyshire SK17 6SW, England,
tel/fax 01298 79598

Photocopiable pupils' sheets are available for
this book, and can be purchased from the
publisher.

Apollo Trust

Richard McNicol founded Apollo Trust in
1977 to explore new ways of involving
pupils of all backgrounds and abilities in
creating and performing their own music
as part of the school curriculum. The
Trust initiated and funded education
projects which involved most of the
British orchestras in their first experience
of practical education work. This initiative
helped to create the momentum that has
established education and development
departments in almost every professional
music establishment in Britain.

Music Explorer
video and guidebook

Educational Television Association Award for Best
Video and Print Resource, 1995

Published by and available from
London Symphony Orchestra,
Barbican Centre, London EC2Y 8DS,
tel 0171-588 1116, fax 0171-374 0127

The London Symphony Orchestra, conducted by Sir
Colin Davis, presents twelve of the finest pieces of
classical music on a 90-minute video, while the
accompanying guidebook by Richard McNicol takes
you through the music – exploring, explaining,
revealing. Music from:

Vivaldi *The Four Seasons*
Bach *Brandenburg Concerto No 2*
Mozart *Eine kleine Nachtmusik*
Beethoven *Symphony No 5*
Mahler *Symphony No 1*
Dvořák *New World Symphony*
Ravel *Mother Goose Suite*
Stravinsky *Firebird Suite*
Ives *Decoration Day*
Holst *The Planets*
Bartók *Concerto for Orchestra*
Shostakovich *Symphony No 10*

Music Explorer
is sponsored by

CORPORATION
OF LONDON

Foundation
for sport
and the arts